The Silence in Marriage

Olamma Maji

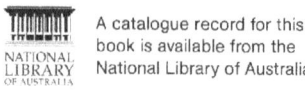
A catalogue record for this book is available from the National Library of Australia

Copyright © 2021 Olamma Maji
All rights reserved.
ISBN-13: 978-1-922343-75-8

Linellen Press
265 Boomerang Road
Oldbury, Western Australia
www.linellenpress.com.au

Dedication

I dedicate the book to Almighty God and to couples experiencing difficulty in their marriages.

Contents

Dedication iii

Contents v

Chapter One 1

Chapter Two - What is marriage? 5

Chapter Three - Why do people marry? 9

Chapter Four - What is Silence in Marriage? 13

Chapter Five 15

    Reasons for the Silence in Marriage 15

    The Dangers of Silence in Marriage 19

    The Right Thing to Do 21

    Is There the Perfect Man or Woman for Me? 25

About the Author 26

Chapter One

She woke up that morning feeling moody, not talking to anyone in the house; she went into the kitchen and filled a cup with water. Her husband moved towards her and gave her a hug. She winced and looked at him in disgust.

He asked, "How was your night?"

In disgust, she silently replied, 'Fine,' and went back into her bedroom. He remained in the living room with their kids, for more than two hours, then went into the bedroom to check on her.

"Darling, what is it?" he asked.

No response.

He moved closer. "Are you okay?"

Still no response.

He put his hands on her shoulder. "Are you okay?"

She pushed his hands away. "Just leave me alone," she said.

Surprised, he needed to figure out what had happened: what had he said or done wrong? He could not think of anything.

"Did anyone offend you?" he asked.

No response.

"Did I offend you?" But he remembered they went to bed happy. *So what has happened?* he thought.

He tried to put his hand on her shoulder again to ask further questions, but she screamed: "Just leave me alone!"

Now he was more worried. What had happened? What could be the problem? He left her alone to give her some space; went to the living room where the kids were. Though he looked at the television, he was not really watching or listening to what was on; he stared into thin air.

"I am really getting tired of this," he said. "How long will I continue to deal with this? She is always angry over nothing. I don't know what I did wrong or who wronged her. As far as I can remember, I have not done anything wrong to her. God help me. This is becoming unbearable."

Throughout that day, Natasha did not talk to her husband. She kept banging doors and frowning.

"I have had enough!" she said to herself. "I go to work, cook, clean up after everyone, take care of the kids … how long will I continue to live this way? If I complain, they will say am nagging," she cried. "Holy Spirit, help me," she muttered.

After three hours, Natasha joined the kids in the living room. She chatted with them then went to the kitchen, cooked and resumed normal conversation with her husband as if nothing had happened earlier.

Her husband asked her again, "What was really wrong with you previously?"

She replied, "Nothing. I am fine. Leave that in the past."

Natasha and Joe have been married for five years now. They have two children together. Natasha is a melancholy and an introvert, while Joe is sanguine and choleric. Natasha most often complains to herself about the state of their home instead of talking to her husband about it. She is not happy. Everything is a trigger for her, which affects their relationship. She feels anytime she complains about what her husband is not doing right, he will say she is nagging, so she resorts to keeping it to herself and mulling it over in her mind.

Joe is so upset. This fateful evening, he clamped his hands on Natasha's shoulders and shook her really hard. "I have had it! I am tired of your mood changing like a chameleon. If you knew you cannot live with someone, why did you get married?"

Not requiring a response, he went on: "One minute you are happy, the next minute you are sad. I am tired of adjusting my mood all the time to suit you. I have had it up to here!" he said, pointing to her neck.

Finally Natasha spoke. "I have had enough of your rubbish! I was done with this hell called 'marriage' two years ago, and if you don't take your hands off me, I will call the police. I am tired of cleaning up after you and the kids; I am tired of being your mother. You do not help me in this house – I cook and do everything. We share the bills, but you work and I work as well, so why can't we share the chores. All you do is go to work, come back and sit on the couch like a king waiting for your slave to serve you. If I have to do everything, then what is your use? I may as well do without you. You are just a useless man – a lazy fool, good-for-nothing! I want you out of the house now, or I will call the police."

For the first time, Joe was silent after listening to his wife's outburst. He dashed into the room, gathered his work clothes and left the house.

Natasha cried so loud and hard, saying to herself, "I have tolerated this for so long … my heart has been so heavy with no one to confide in because I do not want to bring a third party into my marriage. I am tired of being the 'Super wife'. I have been dying silently. I love my husband – I really do not want us to break up. I just wish he could change, that's all. I want him to support me in the home, not leave everything to me. I am breaking down; am weak; am tired." She cried until she fell asleep.

Chapter Two

What is marriage?

According to Google:

Marriage is a union of a man and a woman entered into voluntarily to the exclusion of others.

Another definition says:

Marriage is a formal union and social and legal contract between two individuals that unites their lives legally, economically and emotionally ...

while 'kingdom marriage' is a solemn and public covenant between a man and a woman in the presence of God.

Marriage is an institution established by God, and he is in support of it. That is why the devil is fighting marriage so hard.

The bible says in Genesis 2: 24:

"A man shall leave his father and mother and be joined to his wife and they shall become one flesh".

The devil hates unity, and God loves unity. The devil is trying to make a mockery of God's institution – that is why there is so much divorce in the world. More so, when a man and a woman live in the same house and are having intercourse without any law binding them, it is not considered 'marriage' in the eyes of God.

To buttress this point, in **John 4:16 to 18**, Jesus told the Samaritan woman he met at the well to call her husband. She said I have no husband. Jesus told her she had been with five men and the one she was now with is not her husband.

(Read the full story in *John 4:4 to 24*).

Just because you are having intercourse and living in the same house with someone does not mean you are married. There must be a contract, a vow before God and man.

To the world, 'marriage' is just a mere contract, a piece of paper that can be torn at any time, but to God, marriage is a covenant that is meant to last forever – the two becomes one flesh, in the presence of God husband and wife are seen as one. Vows are meant to be taken seriously because it is done in the sight of God, family and friends. You vow to spend the rest of your life with one person.

More so, because marriage is a covenant you vow, you are supposed to take your time and not rush into it. If you rush in, you may also rush out.

However, although marriage is meant to last forever, there are conditions for divorce, according to the bible.

One can divorce on the ground of infidelity:

> "whosoever divorces his wife for any reason except sexual immorality causes her to commit adultery." Mathew 5:32.

If a wife or husband cheat, they have broken the covenant – they have broken the contract – they have broken their vows which they swore to be faithful to one another forever before God, family and friends.

Another reason for divorce is if one of the partners is an unbeliever – e.g. does not believe in God – and he or she walks away or walks out of the marriage, the other's partner is free. **1 Corinthians 7:17**.

Another reason I add here is if there is abuse: physical, emotional, verbal abuse. For you to be married, you have to be alive first. If you are being abused and you don't walk away, you may end up dead, and your partner will move on to someone else, so it's better to be safe than sorry. Do not sacrifice your destiny on the altar of marriage.

Marriage in all totality is meant for the mature of mind. It involves two adults from different backgrounds, different mentalities, different temperaments, different upbringings. You have to be really ready to venture into it. It's not child's play. It is serious. When you are marrying someone, you are literally telling the person I can give you my life. For example, when a woman is pregnant, her body changes; everything about her changes. Some women die while giving birth to their babies, and while the child belongs to both of you, you are also sacrificing your life, so it has to be worth it – let your partner be worth it.

Chapter Three

Why do people marry?

Here are some major reasons why people marry:

Companionship:

When God created Adam, he said in Genesis 2:18:

> it is not good for man to be alone, I will make him a helper comparable to him. Then he created the woman (Eve) and when Adam saw Eve, he said indeed this the bone of my bone and the flesh of My flesh, she shall be called woman because she was taken out of man. (Genesis 2:23).

Human beings are created as social beings. The word 'social' comes from the Latin word 'socius', meaning *friend*. We are created to interact with others. People marry because they want to have:

- ♥ someone they can spend time with
- ♥ someone they can interact with
- ♥ someone they can confide in
- ♥ someone who will always be there for them
- ♥ someone they can call their own.

For this reason, a man shall leave his father and mother and be joined to his wife and they shall become one flesh (Genesis 2:24). A man or woman leave a form of social interaction with their parent and form another interaction with the husband or wife. Everyone wants that sense of ownership and importance. God saw the need for companionship. That is why he created Adam and Eve (male and female).

Multiplication:

When God created Adam and Eve, he told them to be fruitful and multiply, replenish the earth and subdue it (**Genesis 1:28**). When people marry, they are fulfilling the command of God. They do so because they want to produce their kind, which is their children.

Psalm 127:3 says:

behold children are a heritage from the Lord, the fruit of the womb is a reward;

Verse 5 says:

happy is the man that has his quiver full of them.

Basically, children are gift from God and people get married because they want to have children. Someone might say, 'people also have children without getting married'. Although this is true, the way God deigned it is for people to marry before having children. Even society supports marriage before kids. In the old days, it was a taboo (wrong) to have children or child out of wedlock, but society now sees it as normal, no big deal. But the question I would like to ask you, the reader, does time make the wrong become right? You have the answer.

Love:

This, according to Google, is a set of emotions and behaviours characterised by intimacy, passion and commitment. It involves care, closeness, protection, attraction, affection and trust. People marry because they feel they cannot live without the other person; they want the person with them all the time because they care that much. The best way to show the love they feel is to commit to the person by marrying them.

Sex

Some people marry not because they really want to live in the same house with another adult but because the bible says sex outside marriage is a sin, which is called fornication. To avoid this, they get married.

1 Corinthians 6:18 says:

"flee sexual immorality every sin that a man does is outside the body but he who commits sexual immorality sins against his own body."

Also, because they have been told by family and friends that to have sex you have to be married first, so they get married because they want to do the right thing.

Support.

People marry because they want to pull their resources together. I have heard people say they would like to marry a rich person to get them out of poverty, not necessarily because they love the person, but because they want to benefit from that person. Basically, people marry for financial, material and emotional support. Emotional support is when you marry someone out of pity because you feel when you do, you can support the person to have a better life.

Chapter Four

What is Silence in Marriage?

I define silence in marriage as an act of keeping things to heart that should be addressed and acted on accordingly. Sometimes in marriage, the man or the woman is not happy with an action, behaviour or attitude of the partner. Instead of speaking out, they keep it to themselves and base their response or action over was not voiced. The silence does not necessarily mean they keep malice with the partner when what is meant to be addressed is not. But keeping malice is part of the silence, and when important issues are overlooked the 'silent treatment' often results.

Furthermore, silent build-up over time can result to hatred. Any little trigger brings back memories of past hurts. These can escalate the person's hurt and result in unreasonable behaviour. For example, Natasha in the first chapter did not tell her husband Joe what was bothering her or what he did wrong. She kept bottling things up instead of addressing them. The day she finally spoke out, she insulted him and told him to move out of the house. Different marriages have different issues – one partner might not like the way the other partner presses the toothpaste out from the top of the tube instead the bottom, or not flushing the toilet properly, not doing the dishes after each meal, littering the room with clothes. Instead of speaking out, they keep ignoring it. Whenever the partner repeats the same act the next day, there is a recollection of the same action last week, and the anger builds up. Such continuity may result in an explosive, negative reaction.

In marriage, the little things you overlook are the things that build up and cause harm. You get to a point where you do not have the energy to speak anymore; you overlook things even when you are upset about them. These things, when someone else hears about it, looks like it doesn't make sense but those are the things that lead to divorce.

Chapter Five

Reasons for the Silence in Marriage

One of the reasons I discovered why there is silence in marriage is:

Temperament

Temperament, according to Google, is a person's nature, especially as it permanently affects their behaviour. Actually, I do not like the word 'permanent' for nothing is permanent except God. Everything is subject to change.

There are four major temperaments.

1. Sanguine: these are social, happy, active, lively, fun, funny people. They hate dull or boring places and actions.
2. Choleric: these people like to lead, are goal-oriented, fast, short-tempered and rigid. They are good organisers.
3. Melancholic: these people are moody. They like to analyse things, are quiet thinkers. They are organized.
4. Phlegmatic: these people love to follow the rules. They are peaceful, calm, and flexible.

While a person can have more than one temperament, there is usually the dominate and the recessive.

Adding to temperament is a person's nature or personality. A melancholic man or woman, instead of addressing issues or concerns, will keep it to heart. They will think about the situation so much it will become much bigger than it actually is. They easily keep record of past hurts, which can affect the relationship with their spouse. Most often, based on observation, the melancholic husband or wife usually give the silence – they are often not happy in the marriage because they have a lot on their mind they are worried about. An act or action they do not like from their partners can ruin their entire day. They can get really moody, and address situations on their mind instead of speaking to their partner. They feel their partners should know what is right and act accordingly.

Another Reason:

Partners do not want to be seen as nagging.

Nagging is demanding something from someone, especially something that has already been brought up or discussed. It is a repetitive behaviour in the form of pestering or continuous urging of an individual to complete a previously discussed request or act.

Nobody wants to be called a nagger. The bible says in proverbs 21;9:

it is better to live alone in a tumbled down shack than share a mansion with a nagging spouse.

The term nagging wife, or nagging husband, has been so used that most people in relationships do not want to be addressed in such a manner. Most times, when a partner expresses their concerns or talks about what the other partner is doing wrong, they say the person is nagging. Most people hate such words, so keep silent to avoid being referred to as 'a nagger'.

Here is another reason

Too overwhelmed to deal with situations

When a man or a woman has a lot of responsibilities adding that of the partner can be over-whelming (too much to handle). Sometimes people have more than one job, friends to deal with, extended family and different social activities seeking their attention.

More so, in marriage, many things happen consecutively. For example, the husband shaves without cleaning the sink properly. The wife comes in and says, "Darling, could you please clean after you finish shaving." Then he uses the toilet without flushing properly, then he eats and leaves the plate on the table. She will be too overwhelmed to keep telling him what to do, especially after telling him previously.

Instead of telling him to flush, she will flush the toilet in anger. If the bad habit continues, she becomes stressed out and withdraws.

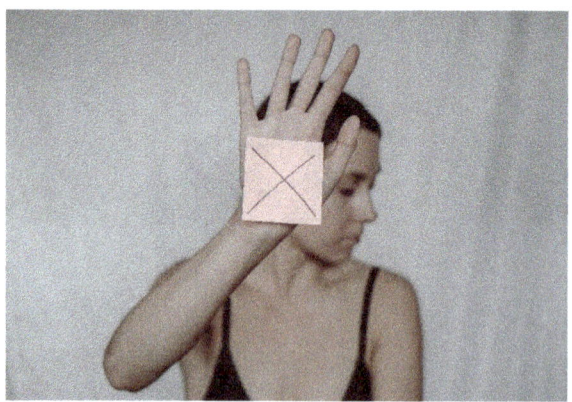

The Dangers of Silence in Marriage

Breakdown in Communication

The number one danger of silence in marriage is the breakdown in communication. Communication is a major tool in marriage. When there is no communication, you do not feel the closeness; it creates distance. The silence in the marriage is already a breakdown in communication.

Sam and Janet are married. Whenever Janet wants to dress up, she brings out all the clothes in her wardrobe and litters the room. Sam does not like that. Being a prim and proper person, he has told Janet several times to clean after herself but he ends up putting the clothes back into the wardrobe as Janet does not really care about the tidiness of their bedroom. Sam is tired of talking. Whenever he comes back from work and sees the room untidy, he gets upset and goes to another room. Even when Janet tries to talk to him, he does not want to talk because he has a lot running through his mind. Because Sam is angry, he will definitely misinterpret whatever Janet says to him at that time because he is not happy.

Unhappiness

If Sam is constantly thinking about what Janet is doing wrong in the marriage, he will never be happy. As a man thinketh so is he, you are what you think over time. His mind will be occupied with the wrongs she does and he will not notice the right things she does. The wrong things can swallow him and he will be living in misery.

Outburst

Outburst is defined as a sudden release of strong emotion.

When Sam cannot take it anymore. There will be a release of negative emotion that can result in hurt, either in words or sometimes physically. Both partners will end up saying hurtful words to each other they can never take back. They can end up hitting or hating each other as a result of what was said, which can finally end in divorce.

The Right Thing to Do

I believe there is silence in every marriage because there are some things that partners are not talking about or are tired of talking. The right thing to do in this situation is:

- ♥ Address concerns immediately
- ♥ Forgive honestly
- ♥ Do not dwell on the past
- ♥ Use the word of God
- ♥ Ask the Holy Spirit to help you

Address concerns immediately

If your partner is doing something that you do not like, call him or her and talk about it. Address the situation because your partner can not read your mind. He/she does not know what you are thinking until you speak of it – they may never know. Remember, both of you are two different individuals from different backgrounds, different temperaments and you may see things differently.

Honestly forgive

Sometimes we, as humans, say we have forgiven people but have not really. You have to learn to forgive your spouse honestly from your heart because if you don't, it will be hard to live with the person, especially if he/she has hurt you really badly. The bible says in Ephesians 4: 26:

be angry and do not sin, do not let the sun go down on your wrath.

Mathew 6: 14 to 15 says:

if you forgive men their trespasses, your heavenly father will also forgive you, but if you do not forgive, neither will your Father forgive your trespasses.

Forgiveness sets you free – it is for your own good. When you fail to forgive, you are actually hurting yourself; you are carrying a whole human being on your mind. Your heart becomes really heavy whenever you think of that person or what they did to you. It brings back pain and hurt that can actually affect you. Marriage cannot work without forgiveness, so if you really want to live with your spouse, forgive truly from your heart because God said so.

Do not dwell on the past

There are people who are fond of recounting wrong done to them in the past by their spouses; they write down any bad thing their spouse does to them and from time to time keep recounting it when their spouse does something they do not like. They give the date and time the spouse offended it in the past. Some recount what their spouse did wrong in their mind each day, even when what they did at present is insignificant. They use the pain of the past to judge them and magnify the situation.

Remember the good times you spent together. Let the good knock off the bad. Luke 9:62 says:

> no one having put his hand to the plow and looking back is fit for the kingdom of God.

God himself does not deal with us based on our past. If God dealt with us based on our past, no one would survive. When we ask for forgiveness, he forgives and throws our sins in the river of forgetfulness. You should learn to forgive, even when you remember past hurt. Do not dwell on it because that affects your judgment and magnifies the situation.

No matter your temperament, do not forget that you are in charge of your life – what you allow becomes. No matter what temperament you are, take the good and work on the bad. It can't control you; you can control it.

Ask the Holy Spirit to help you.

Use the word of God

There is something I have noticed in marriage that I would like to share. When you are praying for God to change someone because you do not like a particular habit or behaviour, which is not necessarily a sin, sometimes the person will not change even after praying for them to. But God will give you the grace to overcome that thing.

Using the previous example, Sam and Janet are married. Janet litters the room with clothes whenever she wants to dress up. This act of Janet gets Samuel so upset that it spoils his day. Now Sam has decided to pray about it and ask for the help of the holy spirit. Janet still did not change. But God has answered Sam's prayer, but in a different way. Sam no longer gets angry when Janet litters the room. He pushes the clothes aside and tells her to arrange it whenever she is up to it. Now, that is the power of the holy ghost.

A sister once shared a testimony with me. She said her husband used to drink a lot with friends; she did not like it. She spoke to him about it but he refused to change. She decided to take it to God in prayer because she knew there is nothing God cannot do. So she prayed.

It took a while, but gradually, her husband did not like going out with his friends anymore. He said his family was more important to him than friends, and gradually, he stopped frequently drinking until he did not remember to drink anymore.

Now, that is the power of prayer. The truth is, there is nothing God cannot do ... all you have to do is to open your mouth and pray. You will be surprised how God will give you the grace to handle the situation. Do not be in a hurry for someone to change; it took them years to form that habit, it may take them a while to change. Know that no-one is perfect. We are all a work in progress – someday we will get there.

Is There the Perfect Man or Woman for Me?

This is the question young people have often asked. In the past, people have often said that there is that one person who is meant for you because Adam said Eve was the bone of his bone and the flesh of his flesh. The question is: if that person that you refer to as the perfect one for you dies, will you remain single forever?

I would like to say that there is no perfect person for anyone. You don't even know if the marriage will work out. You don't even know if the person can be trusted because people change, people pretend; they may just be trying to be as good as possible until they get what they want. I will say though, if you have found the one you want to spend the rest of your life with, just trust God it will work out because you can never fully and truly understand a person. As I said earlier, people change. Anyone can be the right person if both of you see your compatibility. Believe God and make it work.

About the Author

Olamma Maji, a graduate of Mass Communication, came to Western Australia from Nigeria.

A mother of three beautiful children and wife to Apostle Isaiah Maji, founder of JPPM, Olamma wrote this book to encourage everyone work on their differences and to talk to one another about issues in marriage rather than sink into silence until the damage is irreparable.

www.ingramcontent.com/pod-product-compliance
Lightning Source LLC
Chambersburg PA
CBHW071550080526
44588CB00011B/1862